CU[...]
THE GOLDEN
YEARS
IN COLOR

William H. Miller
& Anton Logvinenko

AMBERLEY

For the staff both afloat and ashore of the great Cunard Line

First published 2014

Amberley Publishing
The Hill, Stroud
Gloucestershire, GL5 4EP

www.amberley-books.com

Copyright © William H. Miller & Anton Logvinenko, 2014

The right of William H. Miller & Anton Logvinenko to be identified as the Author of this work has been asserted in accordance with the Copyrights, Designs and Patents Act 1988.

ISBN 978 1 4456 1853 1 (paperback)
ISBN 978 1 4456 1872 2 (ebook)

British Library Cataloguing in Publication Data.
A catalogue record for this book is available from the British Library.

Typeset in 11pt on 12pt Sabon LT Std.
Typesetting by Amberley Publishing.
Printed in the UK.

CONTENTS

FOREWORD

On 4 December 2012, after lunch with Bill Miller in New York on West 44th Street & 9th Avenue, I decided to walk to Lower Manhattan. I wanted to see such significant places as Luxury Liner Row, the Chelsea Piers and Lower Manhattan. There was not a single ship in port that day, but I had colorized photos of the Luxury Liner Row so many times, that I could literally imagine moored here *Queen Mary*, during her repainting in military livery at Pier 90, standing to the left of her *Normandie* at Pier 88; or *Independence* and *Leonardo Da Vinci* at Pier 84. Going down to Lower Manhattan, I reached Chelsea Piers, and sat down on a bench at Pier 54. I saw a container ship passing by the piers and my imagination started immediately painting this picture: '*Olympic* approaching Pier 54 with help of tugs'. It is a special place, which was a witness of almost all great ocean steamers and I felt some connection to the luxury liners of the twentieth century! I think I almost saw the triumphant crowd welcoming a huge ship, heard the music of the orchestra and sounds of pouring champagne. I saw people holding flags of the United Kingdom and the United States, and confetti falling like snow. I wish I could see it all in reality!

After some time, I continued my journey. Passing the wreck of Pier 54 and reaching Pier 45, a sense of deja vu came over me: I felt that I had been here once. Looking up, I noticed Westbeth Artists' Housing; the complex was originally the site of Bell Laboratories (1868–1966). That's it! Two days before, I had colorized the panoramic view of the *Baltic* in New York docks in 1904. I spent four days working on this photo, I had painted each person there, every building and even garbage in the streets. I had studied every pixel of the picture and actually I was living those four days in that place in 1904. And now, 112 years later, I was standing in the same place! It was like a trip back in time! Yes, during colorization of a photo, I seemed to sink in that era, and live it with each work. Of course, I can not know all the color details. Much is known: the color of the shipping company funnels, the color of a hull and superstructure or attractions extant etc. But I can not know for sure, for example, what color were the clothes of people on the deck of a ship or of unknown numbers of buildings in the background. And while I study the colors and fashion clothing the people of that period, and paint all in accordance with the colors of the age, in any job there is some part of creativity and imagination. However, I was pleasantly surprised on 4 December 2012 at Pier 45 in New York, when I noticed that the colors of the buildings, which I had painted at random, and which still survive, in fact it were the same as I imagined.

In this book, Bill Miller and I would like to share with you the experience of this kind of time travel, thanks to its priceless memories and knowledge, as well as my colorized photos.

On the eve of the anniversary of the first transatlantic voyage of the *Britannia*, take a journey with us 175 years ago, and look at the luxury liners of the golden age of Cunard, through the eyes of witnesses. Find yourself in Boston Harbor during the Arctic cold, in January 1844, and feel how the inhabitants of Boston helped little Britain to make her daring escape, and overcame her ice. Meet the *Lusitania* when she completed her first triumphant crossing to New York, and experience the excitement and pride at the time of the launching of the *Queen Mary*, which, with the help of the British people, overcame difficulties in construction during the Great Depression.

You have not seen these grand liners until this point and we invite you to look at the golden years of Cunard in color!

Anton Logvinenko
Kiev, Ukraine

Spring 2014

INTRODUCTION

Cunard! There is no better name in shipping, especially passenger shipping. Capped by their orange-red and black funnels, they have given us more important, historic, record-breaking, notable and simply wonderful ocean liners than any other maritime company. One just has to think of the original *Queens*, the iconic *Queen Mary* and *Queen Elizabeth*, dating from 1936 and 1940, to realize this. They were the most successful pair of Atlantic super liners ever created and, in view of their extraordinary service in the Second World War, the most heroic big liners of all time. A crew member from another great, grand and certainly historic British shipping line, P&O, recalled Cunard in their revived, restored, post-war era, the 1950s. 'They were the ultimate British ship owner. They owned and operated what were the most famous ships under the British flag and in what was then the huge British merchant navy,' he recalled. 'Sometimes, at sea, we'd run into one of the Cunarders, but most especially the *Queens*. We would signal with a loud salute. That was a kind of maritime curtsey to those majestic liners. In the 1950s, every Brit it seemed was proud of the Cunard *Queens*. They were extraordinary.' Another former Cunard crew member in the '50s added, 'To work for Cunard at that time had the greatest prestige. It was like working for the Bank of England. For many seamen, working aboard a Cunarder was the ultimate in assignments.'

The Company was formed by a Canadian, Samuel Cunard, and he was on the Company's very first sailing – aboard the steam paddle-wheeler *Britannia* – when the 1,139-ton vessel departed from Liverpool on 4 July 1840. The 115-passenger ship cast off for Halifax and Boston. Aside from her passengers, she had an important cargo: the mail. Samuel Cunard had been given a British government contract, fixed at £55,000 a year for seven years. The new company was officially named the British & North American Royal Mail Steam Packet Company, but soon became familiarly known as the Cunard Line. Sometimes, it was called 'Mr Cunard's Line'.

As his company grew steadily and prospered, based on great reliability, Samuel Cunard could not have been more pleased. For his great help during the Crimean War (1853–56), for which the Cunard Company provided a veritable armada of liner-troopships, Cunard himself was rewarded with a baronetcy. He was Sir Samuel Cunard until his death on 28 April 1865.

Cunard created successively larger, finer, more innovative ships – as well as periodic record-breakers. Having the 'world's fastest liner' and 'largest liner' was not uncommon to Cunard and its publicists.

Cunard survived two world wars, the Depression of the 1930s and the onslaught of airline competition on the Atlantic in the 1960s. However, it has endured, having been strengthened greatly by its acquisition by the hugely successful Miami-based Carnival Corporation in 1998. This led to the creation of the three largest Cunard liners of all time – the 151,000-ton *Queen Mary 2* (2004), the 90,000-ton *Queen Victoria* (2007) and the 92,000-ton *Queen Elizabeth* (2010).

Cunard has been quite brilliant in creating special events highlighting the Company and its ships, and in fact a rousing salute to all transatlantic liners. Myself, I've been very fortunate – I participated in the gala departure of three *Queens* – *Queen Mary 2*, *Queen Elizabeth 2* and the then brand-new *Queen Victoria* – in New York harbor on a winter's night in January 2008; the sailing of the *Queen Mary 2* and *Queen Victoria*, as the *Queen Elizabeth 2* waited at her Southampton berth, in April 2008; the grand, but also sentimental, final departure from New York of the *Queen Elizabeth 2*, joined by the *Queen Mary 2*, in October 2008; the horn-sounding departure amid colorful fireworks of the *Queen Mary 2*, *Queen Victoria* and the then new *Queen Elizabeth* at New York, again on a crisp winter's night, in January 2011; the rendezvous of the *Queen Mary 2*, *Queen Victoria* and *Queen Elizabeth* for Her Majesty the Queen's Golden Jubilee in June 2012; and the departure from New York on her 200th crossing of the *Queen Mary 2* in July 2013; the overnight visit of the *Queen Victoria* to Liverpool in May 2014 to commemorate the 100th anniversary of the *Aquitania*; and finally, to date, the celebratory 10th anniversary departure of the *Queen Mary 2* from New York in May 2014.

In May 2015, the three current Cunard *Queens* will rendezvous in Liverpool, home to the Company's headquarters until 1968, to celebrate the Company's 175 glorious years. Little more than a month later, the mighty *Queen Mary 2* will recreate the little *Britannia*'s first crossing – from Liverpool to Halifax and Boston (the *Queen* will also continue onward to New York, however). The mood for Cunard in 2015 will be especially festive.

Our book – with Anton's superb colorizations – is a tribute to the great and historic Cunard Line. The whistles are sounding, the lines being cast, the passengers and staff lining the open decks – Happy 175th anniversary, Cunard!

Bill Miller
Secaucus, New Jersey
Spring 2014

BRITANNIA

The very first four Cunarders all had geographical names ending in 'ia', thus starting the famous naming tradition. The first four were the *Britannia* (Britain), *Acadia* (Nova Scotia), *Caledonia* (Scotland) and *Columbia* (America). These paddle-wheel ships only carried 'cabin' passengers – steerage passengers continued to go on sailing packets, which took far longer to reach America. The *Britannia*, built by Robert Duncan & Company at Port Glasgow in 1840, weighed in at 1,139 gross tons and 207 feet in length. She had paddle wheels with side lever engines that could produce a service speed of 9 knots. She could carry 115 cabin passengers. The *Britannia* burned 38 tons of coal a day and, on her first trip, took twelve days and ten hours to cross from Liverpool to Halifax. Afterward, she continued on to Boston.

Cunard became known for its reliability, dependability and safety. However, as with all shipowners, there was the occasional incident. The 2,132-grt *Malta*, built in 1865 and used for a time on the Liverpool–New York run and later to Mediterranean ports from Liverpool, was built to accommodate 639 passengers in total – 46 in cabin class and 593 in third class. She was one of three sisters, the others being the *Aleppo* and *Tarifa*. The 292-foot-long *Malta* met her end tragically, on 15 October 1889, when she was wrecked off Cape Cornwall, the only cape in England. Fortunately, all passengers and crew were saved.

SCYTHIA (1875)

Built at Glasgow in 1875, the 4,500-grt *Scythia* had eight boilers and twenty-four furnaces, and consumed 75 tons of coal per day. Used on the Liverpool–New York service, she could carry over 1,000 tons of cargo as well 1,300 passengers – 200 in first class and 1,100 in steerage.

A sturdy, reliable ship, the 422-foot-long *Scythia* – like most ships – had the occasional mishap. In her maiden year, in July 1875, she broke a propeller blade after striking a whale off Queenstown. Her voyage to America had to be canceled and the ship limped back to Liverpool for repairs.

SERVIA (1881)

Beginning with her maiden voyage from Liverpool to New York in November 1881, the 515-foot-long *Servia* became the largest passenger ship in the world, with the exception of the largely inoperative *Great Eastern*. Cunard emphasized her seagoing safety – she introduced 'light houses' positioned forward on her foc'sle deck, for example.

Cunard was steadily progressive, not only building larger and faster ships, but ones with greater amenities and comforts. The 7,391-grt *Servia*, built at Glasgow in 1881, was not only the first Cunarder with a double bottom, but the first to have electric lighting. She was also Cunard's most comfortable ship yet – carrying her 480 first-class passengers in 202 staterooms. In addition to 500 in third class, she carried a crew of 252, of which 105 were stewards to look after the passengers.

Used as a troopship during the Boer War (being chartered to the British government for 21 shillings per ton per month) beginning in late 1899, the *Servia* endured for over twenty years. After her final sailing from New York in the fall of 1901, she was sold to ship breakers early in the new year, being partially stripped at Barrow-in-Furness and then towed to Preston for final demolition.

Originally to have been called *Sahara*, the twin-funnel, three-masted *Servia* cost almost £257,000 to build.

ETRURIA (1885)

Slightly faster than her sister *Umbria*, the 519-foot-long *Etruria* was dubbed the 'fastest liner on the Atlantic' on several occasions. Cunard was rightfully proud of her. She was used to represent the Company during Queen Victoria's Diamond Jubilee Pageant of Shipping in the Mersey in 1897. With a career lasting only fourteen years, she was soon outmoded by the likes of the far larger *Lusitania* and *Mauretania*, and sold to ship breakers in 1909.

UMBRIA (1884)

The 8,128-grt *Umbria* and her sister *Etruria* were said to be 'the most powerful steamers in the world' when completed in November 1884. When travelling at 21 knots, however, she suffered from severe vibration, but was vibration-free when limited to 19 knots.

Used as a troopship during the Boer War, the *Umbria* was almost blown up at New York in 1903.

Shown overleaf at Liverpool and dressed in flags for Queen Victoria's birthday in 1889, the *Umbria* was retired in 1909. She was sold in the following year for £20,000 to scrappers at Bo'ness in Scotland.

CAMPANIA (1893)

The *Campania* was retired from Cunard service in the spring of 1914, just months before the First World War began, and then was chartered to the Anchor Line for five crossings before filling in for the brand-new *Aquitania*, which was hurriedly taken up for trooping duties. The *Campania* was in fact sold for scrapping by the end of the year, but then acquired by the British Admiralty for conversion to an armed merchant cruiser but with a flight platform on the forward deck. The rebuilt *Campania* could carry 184 seaplanes. Her aft deck was cleared for use by observation balloons. The ship was useful during fleet operations. During a gale in the Firth of Forth on 5 November 1918, however, she broke away from her moorings, slammed into the battleship *Revenge* and then sank.

The *Campania* was a Cunard favorite, a ship of honors and notations, and carried Members of Parliament for Queen Victoria's Diamond Jubilee Review off Spithead.

Built by Fairfield Shipbuilding & Engineering Company at Glasgow, and completed in March 1893, this 12,950-tonner was immediately dubbed the largest and fastest liner afloat. Created also with comfortable quarters, the 620-footer could carry 60 in an intimately luxurious first class, 400 in less fancy second class and, most profitable of all, 1,000 in lower-deck third class. Costing £650,000 to build, and therefore the most expensive Cunarder yet, she captured the prized Blue Riband and later made a fast sailing between Liverpool and New York of five days and nine hours at a speed of 21.59 knots.

LUCANIA (1893)

In June 1901, the *Lucania* was the first Cunarder to be fitted with Marconi wireless. Two years later, in October 1903, she had another distinction: she became the first Cunarder to publish a daily bulletin of news received by radio.

A sister to the *Campania*, the *Lucania* was slightly faster, and broke her sister's record on several occasions, with speeds of well over 21 knots. This scene shows some of her 400 crew.

The *Lucania* was decommissioned, after sixteen years of service, in 1909. Unfortunately, she caught fire on 14 August while laid up in the Huskisson Dock at Liverpool, and then sank. She was later salvaged, however, and sailed under her own power to Swansea for scrapping.

SAXONIA (1900)

Immigration to America boomed, especially in the decade prior to the First World War. Alone, over 1 million arrived each year in New York harbor and, in 1907, had created a record of 12,000 third-class and steerage passengers per day. Cunard had a great part in this – and a profitable one. Alternate entry ports included Boston (seen here), Baltimore, Philadelphia and even Portland, Maine.

Built in 1900, the 14,000-grt *Saxonia* and her twin sister *Ivernia* were noted as having the tallest funnels on the Atlantic – 106 feet from the main deck to the funnel's rim. Designed primarily for the very lucrative migrant trade to America, these ships had seven cargo holds each (for up to 14,000 tons of cargo) as well as 164 passengers in first class, 200 second class and 1,600 third class. Costing £400,000 each, they were also designed with provision for war and could carry up to 4,000 troops. Designed for the Liverpool–Boston run, they also made sailings from Liverpool to New York and later in Cunard's alternate Mediterranean service between Trieste or Fiume and New York.

Seen again at Boston, the 600-foot-long *Saxonia* was called to war duties in the late summer of 1914, but for an unusual purpose: she was used to house German prisoners of war while anchored in the Thames. While the *Ivernia* was later torpedoed and sunk in the Mediterranean, the *Saxonia* resumed wartime service on the Atlantic, survived and then ran a Hamburg–New York migrant service between 1920 and 1924. She ended her days at a scrapyard near Rotterdam in 1925.

CARPATHIA (1902)

Largely unnoticed, she would become, however, a very famous ship. On 15 April 1912, she was the only rescue ship in the sinking of the *Titanic*. In all, this little, very heroic Cunarder rescued the 705 survivors. She is seen in this view, heading for New York with *Titanic* lifeboats aboard. Being torpedoed in July 1918, the *Carpathia* lives on in the deep, overall and very enduring interest in the *Titanic* tragedy.

A slightly smaller, modified version of the earlier *Saxonia* and her sister *Ivernia*, the 13,600-grt *Carpathia* was designed largely for ordinary migrant service. She had accommodations for 204 second-class and 1,500 third-class passengers (the latter in 486 cabins and the remainder in dormitories).

The *Carpathia* divided her services by season: summers between Liverpool and New York; winters between Trieste and New York. She occasionally called at other ports such as Valletta on Malta.

The *Carpathia* was refitted in 1905 so as to be more suitable to Cunard's Mediterranean passenger service. Her berthing was arranged as 100 first class, 200 second class and 2,250 third class. On her sailings between Trieste and New York, a call at Ponte Delgada in the Azores was added.

CARONIA (1905)

The 19,524-grt *Caronia* was commissioned in February 1905 as the biggest Cunarder yet. She was the first of an important pair of liners in another way. Cunard wanted to test the newly devised steam turbine for the far larger *Lusitania* and *Mauretania* and so experimented – the *Caronia* would use traditional steam quadruple-expansion engines while her twin sister, the *Carmania*, would use the new geared turbines. The *Carmania* proved more efficient as well as faster.

Used on the Liverpool–New York run, the *Caronia* – which could carry 300 first-class, 350 second-class and 1,100 third-class passengers – is seen here off Plymouth en route to America. In January 1906, with her capacity specially reduced to 400, all-first class, the 675-foot-long ship made a special detour: a long, luxury cruise from New York through the Mediterranean. It was a huge success, and the beginning of Cunard's interest in cruising, especially long, luxurious ones. In the 1920s, the *Caronia* was especially popular for her seven-night cruises between New York and Havana. Minimum fare was $40.

The *Carmania* and her sister were considered to be very handsome-looking liners, with twin masts and twin funnels. They were dubbed 'the pretty sisters'.

CUNARD LINE.

"CARONIA" and "CARMANIA."

THIRD CLASS COVERED PROMENADE.

THIRD CLASS DINING ROOM.

THIRD CLASS SITTING ROOM.

THIRD CLASS FOUR-BERTH ROOM.

CARMANIA (1905)

The *Carmania*, seen on the previous page in the Clyde, is perhaps best remembered for her wartime encounter with German liner *Cap Trafalgar* in September 1914. A battle ensued between the two liners, both then serving as armed merchant cruisers. The *Carmania* was hit twenty-nine times and caught fire, but survived; the *Cap Trafalgar* was badly damaged and sank.

Drawing Room: CUNARD R.M.S. "CARMANIA" – "CARONIA"

LUSITANIA (1907)

The *Lusitania* and *Mauretania* were Cunard's first super liners of the twentieth century. They were record-breaking in every way – largest, longest, fastest and, to some, the most luxurious yet to sail the Atlantic. The two liners differed in some ways, however – the upper decks of the 790-foot-long *Lusitania* were less cluttered and therefore her four funnels seemed taller.

Seen arriving in New York for the first time in September 1907, the 31,550-ton *Lusitania* – built by John Brown & Company Limited at Clydebank, Scotland – could carry 563 in luxurious first class, 464 in less extravagant second class and then 1,186 in third class. She had a crew of just over 800.

Operating with a generous subsidy from the British government, the *Lusitania* as well as the *Mauretania* were highly successful, very popular and much loved by both passengers and staff. The *Lusitania* was fondly dubbed 'the Lucy'.

The *Lusitania* and *Mauretania* were purposely designed – they were Atlantic liners in peacetime and either troopships or armed merchant cruisers in time of war.

When completed, the *Lusitania* captured the coveted Blue Riband with a crossing between Queenstown and Sandy Hook of four days, nineteen hours and fifty-two minutes for an average speed of 23.99 knots.

Kriegsschauplatz auf den engl. Gewässern: Die „Lusitania" torpediert.
Serie 11/9

The *Lusitania* is immortal – one of the great liners in maritime history. Kept on a sort of commercial service between Liverpool and New York even as the war unfolded, she became one of its greatest casualties. She was torpedoed off the Irish coast by a German U-boat on 7 May 1915, and then quickly sank, with the horrific loss of 1,198 lives. So enraged, this single tragedy was said to have drawn America into that 'war to end all wars'.

R.M.S. "LUSITANIA."

SUNDAY, APRIL 26th, 1908.

- - MENU. - -

Oysters on the Half Shell
Hors d'œuvres

Green Turtle
Brett—Hollandaise Sauce
Sweetbreads—Toulouse
Potage a la Marie Stuart
Whiting a la Maître d'Hotel
Duckling en Compote

Sirloin and Ribs of Beef
Roast Surrey Capon
Roast Loin of Veal
Ox Tongue—Spinach
Saute of Mushrooms   Baked Tomatoes   Boiled Rice
Potatoes—Boiled New. Bordelaise. and Mashed
Roast Haunch of Venison
Salad

Plum Pudding   Genoise Parisienne   Rhubarb Tart
Gelee au Champagne
Ice Cream
Dessert

Tea   Coffee
Choice Cold Meats

MAURETANIA (1907)

Initially, Cunard and their designers thought of grouping the four funnels aboard the *Mauretania* as well as the *Lusitania*, like the big German liners, their arch-rivals. However, four evenly spaced funnels aboard the Cunarders produced two of the most handsome four-stackers, as well as two of the best-looking liners, of the twentieth century. The late Frank Braynard, one of the greatest maritime historians, authors and artists, once said, 'These Cunarders were classic beauties – the kind that old sailors of today look back upon with great nostalgia.'

The *Mauretania* was one of the most beloved of all Atlantic liners, a favorite to thousands of travelers, and the fastest ship in the world for twenty-two years. She held the prized Blue Riband from 1907 until 1929.

The 31,938-grt *Mauretania* was a member of that very select group of big liners known as the 'floating palaces'. Her interiors represented the very best in design and quality – from French Renaissance to English country. The first-class main lounge, as an example, featured a large domed skylight, a marble fireplace, highly polished woods and the thickest carpeting. The dining room was a two-deck-high affair, while the Verandah Café featured wicker chairs and 'new' linoleum flooring. A week's crossing aboard the *Mauretania* in first class could cost as much £200.

Following their completion, both the *Mauretania* and the *Lusitania* had frequent refits – in particular, adjustments to their machinery and propellers – so as to improve their performance. Cunard was even hoping to attain a five-day passage between Liverpool and New York, but it remained at six days.

The *Mauretania* was one of the most heroic ships of the First World War. Called to duty in 1914, she was repainted in gray, and made three voyages out to Gallipoli, heavily loaded with soldiers. Later, she was repainted in red and white, and used as a hospital ship. On one voyage from the Mediterranean homeward to Liverpool, she had 6,298 wounded aboard. In 1916, she was again repainted – this time in 'dazzle paint', a series of geometric shapes that allowed her to blend with the sea and escape the treacherous U-boats.

To the mostly American and Canadian soldiers who came aboard in 1916–18, the 790-foot-long *Mauretania* was affectionately dubbed 'the Maury'.

While still hugely popular in the 1920s, the Depression of the early '30s caused problems on the Atlantic, especially for aging dowagers such as the *Mauretania*. Business plummeted – 1 million passengers crossed in 1930, but there were just ½ million five years later. The *Mauretania* was soon sent mostly on cruises – to the Bahamas, the Caribbean and sometimes on longer jaunts around the Mediterranean. She also made bargain cruises – $10 overnight trips 'to nowhere' from New York and three-day weekend sailings up to Halifax and back for $40. In 1932, she was even repainted in all white, giving her a more tropical, cooler appearance.

LUNCHEON

ON THE
OCCASION OF THE
INSPECTION OF THE
TURBINE MACHINERY AND BOILERS
FOR THE
CUNARD ROYAL MAIL STEAMER "MAURETANIA"
AT THE WORKS OF
THE WALLSEND SLIPWAY AND ENGINEERING CO. LIMITED.

WALLSEND   20th Sept. 1906

The end for the twenty-seven-year-old *Mauretania* came in September 1934. She left New York, a sentimental occasion, for the last time on 26 September, the same day that the *Queen Mary* was being launched in Scotland. Indeed, it was a symbolic day – the old and the new. While a perfect candidate for use as a floating museum or even hotel, she sat at the Southampton Docks for a time; her furnishings and fittings were auctioned off, and the ship made a melancholy last sailing up to Rosyth in Scotland and the breakers.

FRANCONIA (1911)

The 18,150-grt *Franconia* and her sister *Laconia* were designed purposely for the Liverpool–Boston run. In 1913, they introduced a call at Fishguard on their crossings, a stop Cunard felt would be an added convenience to some passengers. The 625-foot-long liner is seen here in dry dock on the Tyne.

The Boston service was very popular, especially with westbound Irish immigrants, who boarded at Queenstown (later Cobh). The *Franconia* is seen here passing Castle Island in Boston harbor.

Unfortunately, both the *Franconia* and *Laconia* were losses in the First World War. The five-year-old *Franconia* was torpedoed and sunk off Malta on 4 October 1916; the *Laconia* was torpedoed and sunk as well, but off Ireland on 25 February 1917. In all, Cunard lost twenty-two ships, many of them almost brand new, in that war.

BERENGARIA (1921)

When she was completed in the spring of 1913, the *Imperator* of the Hamburg America Line was the biggest liner yet. She weighed in at over 52,000 tons and was 919 feet in length. She could carry as many as 4,594 passengers, plus 1,180 crew. She sat out the First World War at Hamburg, but then was seized by the Allies and chartered briefly by Cunard for use on the Atlantic run as the RMS *Imperator*. By 1921, however, she was officially sold, renamed *Berengaria* and refitted. She became one of the most popular liners of the 1920s, carrying tycoons, starlets, royalty and only 'the smartest dogs' in her top-deck kennels. Some millionaires so preferred the *Berengaria* that they booked suites aboard her years in advance.

Despite her German heritage, the *Berengaria* was the Cunard flagship and largest member of the Company's 'Big Three', the others being the *Mauretania* and *Aquitania*, on the express run between Southampton and New York. They were in direct competition with White Star Line's *Majestic*, *Olympic* and *Homeric*.

Used for inexpensive cruises in the Depression years of the early 1930s, and dubbed the 'Bargain-area', she still established records. In September 1935, at Southampton, she had a record turnaround of 13¼ hours, during which time more than 1,000 passengers and their baggage were handled, over 4,000 bags of mail processed, 7,000 tons of fuel pumped into her bunkers, 1,000,000 gallons of fresh water pumped into her tanks and 30 tons of ship's stores taken aboard.

AQUITANIA (1914)

The *Aquitania* was a follow-up to the highly successful *Lusitania* and *Mauretania* of 1907. She would be larger and possibly more beautifully decorated; she was on the Liverpool–New York express run, but wasn't expected to be quite as fast. She, too, had military overtones – she could be used, so felt the Admiralty, as a large armed merchant cruiser in time of war. Launched in May 1913, at the John Brown yard on the Clyde, she was commissioned a year later, in May. The war started that August. She was eventually used as a troopship, hospital ship and, very briefly, as an armed merchant cruiser. When she resumed something of commercial service in December 1919, she was based at Southampton, which had just replaced Liverpool for the express liner run to and from New York.

Many thought the 45,647-ton *Aquitania* was the most handsome and well balanced of all the four-stackers. She was quickly dubbed the 'Ship Beautiful'. She was long and sleek, and each of her four funnels worked (unlike many other three- and four-funnel liners of the day). Even her name was very appealing – *Aquitania* was the ancient Roman province in south-west France.

Seen on the next page at the Ocean Dock at Southampton with another, far smaller Cunarder, the 13,900-grt *Andania* (built in 1922), the 901-foot-long *Aquitania* was one of the most popular Atlantic liners of the twenties and thirties. Not only was she a great favorite with the Hollywood set (silent film kings and queens were photographed at her rails on an almost weekly basis), but there came royalty, government officials, inventors, great athletes and more. In addition, she seemed to have a particular appeal – 'a unique onboard chemistry', according to one passenger – to those travelers who did favor one particular ship. She sailed in weekly tandem with the larger *Berengaria* and the speed champion *Mauretania*.

Times were changing and ships had to adapt. When the US government began its immigration quota system in 1924, third-class traffic diminished. Lower-deck quarters had to be improved, even if slightly, for a new generation of bargain tourists – schoolteachers, students, secretaries and others. During a refit in 1926, the accommodation aboard the *Aquitania* were suitably adjusted: from 618 to 610 in first class, 614 to 950 in second class and, most noted of all, from 1,998 third class to 640 in the renamed tourist class. Periodically, she was improved as well – being fitted with a sound cinema during a 1933 refit, for example. She made the occasional headline, such as when she ran aground near Southampton; she was kept in place for twenty-six hours and then finally freed with the help of no fewer than eleven tugs. In the view overleaf of New York's 'Luxury Liner Row', from August 1939, war is just days away, and much of the Atlantic liner trade will come to a screeching halt. The *Bremen* is at the top, the *Normandie* is already laid up, then the *Aquitania* and, at the bottom, Italy's *Roma*.

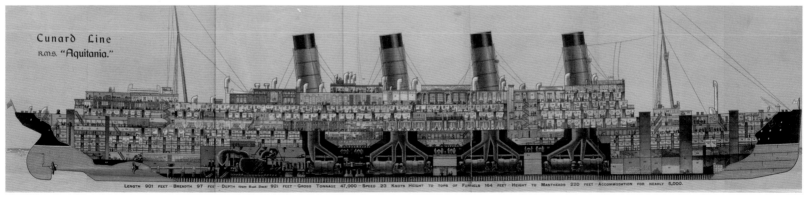

Cunard Line
R.M.S. "Aquitania."

LENGTH 901 FEET – BREADTH 97 FEET – DEPTH (from Boat Deck) 92½ FEET – GROSS TONNAGE 47,000 – SPEED 23 KNOTS HEIGHT TO TOPS OF FUNNELS 164 FEET – HEIGHT TO MASTHEADS 220 FEET – ACCOMMODATION FOR NEARLY 5,000.

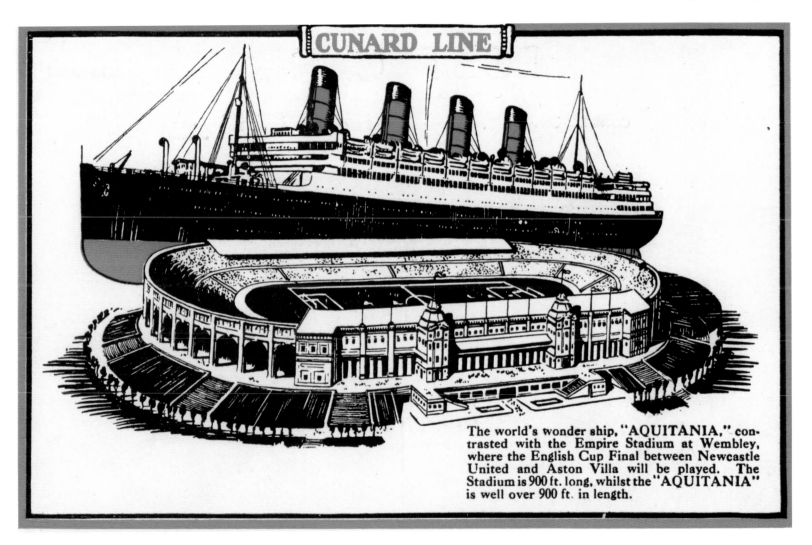

CUNARD LINE

The world's wonder ship, "AQUITANIA," contrasted with the Empire Stadium at Wembley, where the English Cup Final between Newcastle United and Aston Villa will be played. The Stadium is 900 ft. long, whilst the "AQUITANIA" is well over 900 ft. in length.

The *Aquitania* had been a great favorite with Cunard – especially for crossings, but also on cruises from three nights up to Halifax from New York to eight weeks around the Mediterranean. After 1936, she was paired with the brand new *Queen Mary* (and another Atlantic dowager, the *Berengaria*). It was planned that the *Aquitania* would be retired by 1940, just as the *Queen Elizabeth* was commissioned. These plans quickly changed, however, after the war in Europe began on 3 September 1939. Quickly painted over in gray, the *Aquitania* began duties in her second world war. Seen here in New York in October 1939, with the Italian super liner *Rex* berthed at adjacent Pier 92, the *Aquitania* was certified to carry as many as 7,724 wartime passengers, most of them being soldiers.

The *Aquitania* carried returning soldiers, refugees and war brides on the so-called 'diaper run' in 1945–48. Afterward, she was returned to the Company, hastily refitted, repainted in Cunard colors and pushed out on an 'austerity service' between Southampton and Halifax, carrying mostly immigrants, displaced persons and some of the Allied occupation troops. There were twelve such voyages in 1948, and a further thirteen during 1949. She was not restored to her magnificent self, however. When her operating certificate expired in December 1949, given her old age (she had been sailing continuously for almost thirty-six years), the end for the last of the four-stackers had come. She had completed 443 voyages and steamed 3 million miles when she was sold to scrappers and broken up at Faslane in the winter of 1950.

SAMARIA

Following the First World War, Cunard sensibly opted to rebuild –
one combination passenger-cargo ship (the unsuccessful *Albania*),
five 20,000-ton liners, six 14,000-ton 'A Class' liners and one
'odd man out', the *Tyrrhenia* (soon renamed *Lancastria*).

The 19,597-grt *Samaria*, completed in April 1922, was
the second of the 20,000-ton class. The previous ship was
the identical *Scythia*. As intended, the first three were for the
Liverpool–New York run, while the latter two were thought
to be used on the Liverpool–Boston run. These ships were very
practical – they carried over 2,200 passengers in three classes,
had space for considerable cargo, and could be adapted for off-
season, one-class cruising as well. The *Samaria* made several early
World Cruises for Cunard, and was, in 1924, the first Cunarder
to pass through the Panama Canal. She would also cruise from
Liverpool, London and Southampton. After strenuous service in
the Second World War as a troopship, the *Samaria* was restored,
but for the Southampton–Quebec City service. Her quarters
were much changed by then, however, catering for 250 in first
class and 650 in tourist class. Before going to the scrappers in the
summer of 1956, the 625-foot-long *Samaria* represented Cunard
among the 260 vessels at Queen Elizabeth II's Coronation Naval
Review on 15 June 1953.

FRANCONIA (1923)

Among the thirteen new passenger ships ordered by Cunard after the First World War, the sisters *Franconia* and *Carinthia* – intended for North Atlantic service – went on to become two of the most popular cruise ships of the 1930s. They were noted for their long, luxurious voyages – one- to five-month-long voyages. The *Franconia* was delivered to Cunard in June 1923, the *Carinthia* in the summer of 1925.

Seen here at Sydney during one of her early 150-night World Cruises, the *Franconia* and her sister were frequently refitted and improved, especially in consideration of the increasingly demanding American cruise public. With up to 2,200 berths in three classes, the *Franconia* was restyled to carry as few as 400 all first-class travelers in a club-like setting. After the Depression began, in October 1929, more and more ships – including the likes of the legendary *Mauretania* – turned to 'escapist' cruising, either on those long-haul trips for millionaires or on very short runs to, say, Bermuda or Havana for as little as $10 a day. The *Franconia* and her sister were made more competitive – most of her cabins were fitted with private bathroom facilities, and improvements were made to her ventilation system.

In another view at Sydney, the *Franconia* – later repainted in heat-resistant all white – was one of the most popular World Cruise ships of her time. For her January 1937 circumnavigation, for example, Cunard advertised the glamorous voyage as being the equivalent of 1½ times around the world. In 144 days, she would travel over 35,000 miles. Outbound from New York, her ports of call included Trinidad, Brazil, St Helena, South Africa, Madagascar, the Seychelles, India, Ceylon, the Straits Settlements, Malaya, Siam, Java, Bali, the Philippine islands, China, Korea, Japan, the Hawaiian islands, California and Panama. Fares began at $1,900.

ALAUNIA

Seen arriving in a moody fog, the *Alaunia* was one of six smaller 'A Class' Cunarders built purposely for service to Eastern Canada. The group consisted of the *Andania* (1922), *Antonia* (1922), *Ausonia* (1922), *Aurania* (1924), *Alaunia* (1925) and *Ascania* (1925). With seven holds for cargo, these practical ships of 1,400 tons each could carry up to 1,700 passengers – 500 in first class and 1,200 in third class. They were each manned by a crew of 270.

Departing from Southampton, the *Alaunia* was lost in the Second World War, being torpedoed and sunk off Iceland in June 1940. Only the *Ascania* resumed Cunard service after the war, being used on the Liverpool–Montreal run until scrapped in 1957. The others were purchased by the Admiralty and spent their latter years in use as naval repair ships.

LANCASTRIA

Built as the *Tyrrhenia* in 1922, her name was never popular with passengers, crew or even the notorious Liverpool dockers, so it was changed to *Lancastria* within two years. Used on the North Atlantic, she was, like many other ships, hard hit in the Depression years, and so was painted all white and sent on, often inexpensive 'escapist', cruises. She cruised from Southampton as well as Liverpool and London, and is seen here on a Northern Cruise at Lerwick in the remote Shetland Islands. The date is 17 July 1937.

Shown here in the Kiel Canal during a Baltic cruise from London, happy days for the 16,243-grt, 1,846-passenger *Lancastria* turned far more serious and then tragic once the Second World War started in September 1939. The 578-foot-long ship was used for the mass evacuation of France on 17 June 1940. As the French surrendered to the advancing Nazi armies, the *Lancastria* arrived at Saint-Nazaire and took on over 5,000 evacuees, including great numbers of women and children. Shortly afterward, she was attacked by enemy bombers. The first bomb went through her funnel and then exploded down in the engine room. Two others hit the cargo holds, and blew out the sides of the ship. Survivors reported that the ship 'jumped' out of the water. She sank within twenty minutes, with the loss of at least 3,000 or possibly as many as 5,000. The tragedy, one of the worst in maritime history, was considered by many, including Winston Churchill himself, to be so demoralizing that full details were withheld for all the war, until the summer of 1945.

CARINTHIA (1925)

Built at Barrow-in-Furness by Vickers, the 625-foot-long *Carinthia* was to have been the *Servia*, but the name was changed well before launching. Commissioned in August 1925, she is seen here at anchor in New York's Lower Bay before proceeding to her berth at Pier 54 in Manhattan.

Shown in the early 1930s and framed by the famed Harbour Bridge, the *Carinthia* is berthed at Sydney during one of her long World Cruises. In 1930, she was chartered by Cunard to the Furness-Bermuda Line for several months on the New York–Bermuda run. Furness had just lost their liner *Bermuda* to fire, and needed a fast replacement. In 1935, the *Carinthia* – like her sister *Franconia* – was repainted in all white.

Carinthia was among the six ships lost by Cunard during the Second World War, being torpedoed by a Nazi U-boat off the Irish coast on 6 June 1940. Six crewmen were killed instantly by the explosion onboard. Nevertheless, while the 20,000-ton liner was clearly doomed, she stayed afloat for thirty-five hours, long enough for all others aboard to be rescued.

BRITANNIC

In February 1934, Cunard merged with a long-time rival, the financially ailing White Star Line. The company was restyled as Cunard-White Star Limited. Cunard inherited ten liners from White Star: *Majestic*, *Olympic*, *Homeric*, *Britannic* (seen here arriving at Boston), *Georgic*, *Laurentic*, *Doric*, *Calgaric*, *Albertic* and *Adriatic*.

Completed in 1930, the 27,600-grt *Britannic* was, in fact, the last survivor of the White Star Line. After the Second World War, she sailed on the Liverpool–Cobh–New York run for almost ten months of the year and then made a long, sixty-day cruise from New York around the entire Mediterranean each winter. When this 712-foot-long liner was retired in December 1960, and sold to ship breakers in Scotland, she was the last surviving liner from White Star.

MAJESTIC

Another noted liner acquired by Cunard in the merger was the 56,551-grt *Majestic*, the largest liner in the world from 1922 until the advent, thirteen years later, of the 79,280-grt *Normandie* in

1935. The 956-foot-long *Majestic* was to have been the *Bismarck*, the third of Hamburg America Line's giant liners built between 1913 and 1915. Completion of the *Bismarck* was stopped due to the outbreak of the First World War and then, after the armistice, she was given to the British as reparations. More specifically, she was assigned to White Star due to the loss of the 48,000-ton *Britannic*, which was mined in 1916. Finally complete in March 1922, the *Majestic* received great publicity because she was the world's largest ship of any kind. A great honor befell the liner in August 1922 when Their Majesties King George V and Queen Mary visited her during Cowes Week. Hereafter, she was very popular on the Southampton–New York express run, but increasingly fell on hard times during the Depression of the early thirties. When Cunard acquired the 23½-knot ship in February 1934, she was streaked in rust, sailing half-full and running occasional cheap cruises as an alternative. She was, however, soon earmarked for disposal. She was sold to scrappers in May 1936, just as the new *Queen Mary* was being added to the fleet, but then soon resold to the British Admiralty for use as a moored boys' training ship at Rosyth in Scotland. She might have actually been revived for troop service after war erupted on 3 September 1939, but caught fire on the 29th, was badly damaged and then sank in an upright position. Resold to the breakers, she was fully dismantled where she lay at Rosyth by 1943. This view shows the *Majestic* in her heyday, being dry-docked in Boston, where the US Navy had one of the only graving docks in the United States capable of handling such a large ship.

QUEEN MARY (1936)

Cunard's, and therefore Britain's, place on the prestigious and highly competitive North Atlantic run had to be reaffirmed and strengthened by the late 1920s. Germany had added their giant and very fast *Bremen* and *Europa*, Italy was planning what would become the *Rex* and *Conte di Savoia*, and then, most worrisome of all, the French were constructing the innovative *Normandie*. Cunard planned two super liners, the first of which would be named *Victoria*. Estimated at nearly 80,000 tons, it would be the largest and fastest Cunarder yet. She was ordered from the John Brown shipyard at Clydebank. While the first plates were laid in December 1930, the havoc of the Depression reached the Clyde a year later, in December 1931. Construction was halted for 2½ years as the great hull sat untouched – lonely, silent and guarded by a small security team. Work resumed in April 1934 and months later, in September, the 1,018-foot-long liner was launched as the *Queen Mary*. Queen Mary herself did the naming before thousands at the shipyard; it was an event broadcast through Britain and its vast empire.

The *Queen Mary* as completed carried 776 in cabin class (the equivalent of first class), 784 tourist class and 579 third class. In her post-war years, this was amended to 711 first class, 707 cabin class and 577 tourist class.

The 80,776-grt *Queen Mary* left the Clyde in March 1936 for trials, and then set off in May on her maiden crossing from Southampton to New York. The new Cunard flagship excelled – she made worldwide headlines, became the world's fastest liner and was listed as the world's largest as well. Although she lacked the glitter and high fascination that surrounded the *Normandie*, she was an extremely successful ship from the start – averaging 98 per cent capacity – and more than pleased her owners. It seems the only real concern was her tendency to roll at sea. A crew man once said, 'The *Queen Mary* could roll the milk out of a cup of tea!'

Typical of all the great liners, the *Queen Mary* was a ship of fascinating interest and detail. The 140-ton rudder had a door in its side so that it could be inspected internally while in dry dock. There were 16-ton anchors, each with 990 feet of anchor chain. There were 151 watertight compartments, 10 million rivets, 2,000 portholes and windows, 2,500 square feet of glass and 257,000 turbine blades. The three whistles weighed 1 ton each and could be heard for 10 miles. There were 700 clocks and 600 phones onboard. One report described Cunard's growth, calling it the leading transatlantic company, from an entire fleet totaling 81,126 tons in 1876 to one in which a single ship weighed 81,000 tons a century later.

In the *Queen Mary*'s early years, in 1937, fares started at $282 in cabin (first) class, $149 in tourist (cabin) class and $93 in third (tourist) class. On the Southampton–Cherbourg–New York express run, she was teamed with two veterans, the *Berengaria* and *Aquitania*.

The *Queen Mary* was rather abruptly laid up in September 1939 in the safe waters of New York. She is seen opposite, berthed at Pier 90, at the foot of West 50th Street, in company with the *Normandie* and *Aquitania*. The *Mary* was supposedly awaiting the 'quick end' to the war in Europe, but that end was far off. She was repainted in gray and then, in the following March, sat across from the newly arrived *Queen Elizabeth*. The two giant *Queens* met for the first time. The *Mary* soon went off to war – in April, without formal notice, she slipped off on a rainy afternoon bound for Sydney.

The *Queen Mary* was decommissioned from war duties in September 1946 and sent to the John Brown yard for refitting. On 31 July of the following year, she resumed service between Southampton and New York (with a stop at Cherbourg in each direction) and for the first time was joined commercially by the *Queen Elizabeth*. The two-ship team, a long-held project of Cunard, delayed by seven years because of the war and with a weekly departure in each direction, was the first of its kind in Atlantic liner history. The pairing created the most economically successful team of ships ever built. For the next fifteen years or so, the *Queen Mary* and *Queen Elizabeth* (the former always being the slightly more popular) were superbly profitable to Cunard.

In the post-war years and especially the 1950s, the *Queens* were immensely popular, and were often booked a year in advance. Fares for their five-day crossings in the mid-1950s started at $400 in first class, $250 in cabin class and $175 in tourist class. In this summertime view at New York, the *Queen Mary* is outbound, having just departed from Pier 90 – while behind (from left to right) are the *Kungsholm*, *Britannic*, *Mauretania*, *New York* and the very front of the *United States*.

Right: Arriving in New York in June 1945, the return of the *Queen Mary* on that date and with 15,000 troops aboard was symbolic of the end of the Second World War in Europe. Used as the biggest and most valiant Allied troopships, the *Queens* carried over 2 million passengers in wartime. The *Mary* established the record for the greatest number of souls carried in a single ship, in July 1943, with 16,683 on board.

Left above: Grand gathering! Cunarders, especially the *Queens*, were usually part of the great gatherings of liners at New York, along 'Luxury Liner Row'. This view in later years, dated September 1957, shows (from top to bottom) the *Independence*, *United States*, *Olympia*, *Flandre*, *Mauretania*, *Queen Mary* and *Britannic*.

Left below: As the airlines took over the transatlantic passenger trade in the 1960s, the *Queens* became dated, tired and uneconomic. The *Mary* was the first to go, in September 1967, after over 1,000 crossings. While she might have been scrapped or become a migrant ship to Australia, a casino at Gibraltar or even a high school in Brooklyn, she was sold to the City of Long Beach, California, for $3½ million, and rebuilt as a moored hotel, museum and collection of restaurants and shops. In 2012, she marked forty years in this role.

Opposite page: Sailing day! This scene is dated April 1959 – the *Mauretania* has just sailed, while in the background (from left to right) are the *Media*, *Queen Mary*, *Ivernia*, *Liberte*, *United States* and *Giulio Cesare*.

MAURETANIA (1939)

As Cunard was building the giant *Queen Mary* and *Queen Elizabeth* in the 1930s, there was, Company directors felt, the need for a slightly smaller and slower 'relief ship' – a liner that could fill in for one of the *Queens*, if they were being refitted or dry-docked. Laid down in May 1937 at the Cammell Laird shipyard at Birkenhead, near Liverpool, the new 35,600-tonner took her name from a well-known previous liner, the beloved speed champion *Mauretania*. Cunard publicists did feel, however, that the new, 772-foot liner might be overshadowed by the legendary record of her predecessor. Because the new liner would have the greatest amount of both daylight and fresh air to fill her inner accommodation, she was dubbed the 'Sunshine Ship'. This projected a special, innovative image for the new liner.

The 'new' *Mauretania* arrived in New York, on a special crossing from Liverpool, on her maiden arrival in June 1939.

In her maiden summer of 1939, the *Mauretania* was assigned to sailings between London (Tilbury), Southampton, Le Havre and New York, joining the sisters *Britannic* and *Georgic*. The new *Mauretania* was, in fact, the largest liner to use the London Docks.

The *Mauretania* was one of the first liners to be called to duty, in September 1939, as war in Europe erupted. Painted over in gray, she was soon off to military service, carrying up to 8,000 soldiers per sailing, and first operating across the Indian Ocean in company with the similar-sized *Nieuw Amsterdam* and *Île de France*. Later used on the North Atlantic troop shuttle, the *Mauretania* had a valiant record by war's end. This included circling the globe on one voyage in little more than eighty-one days.

The *Mauretania* was one of Cunard's most popular Atlantic liners after the war, in the late 1940s and throughout the 1950s.

In winter, she cruised the Caribbean, mostly on two- and three-week voyages from New York. However, after the first jet aircraft flew the London–New York route in October 1958, demand changed quickly. In six months, the airlines had two-thirds of all passenger traffic; by 1963, they had 98 per cent. Ships such as the aging *Mauretania* struggled, running an unsuccessful Mediterranean–New York service as well as more cruises. Sometimes her sailings were canceled due to too few passengers. The 772-foot-long liner sailed off to the breakers in late 1965.

QUEEN ELIZABETH (1940)

The second giant Cunard *Queen* might have been called *King George V*, but instead it was named *Queen Elizabeth*. Laid down in December 1936 at the John Brown yard at Clydebank, the 83,673-grt liner – the world's largest ship – was launched on 27 September 1938. Weighing 40,000 tons at launching, the liner was named by Her Majesty Queen Elizabeth, accompanied by Princess Elizabeth (later Queen Elizabeth II) and Princess Margaret. Actually, the 1,031-foot hull began to move down the ways and into the River Clyde before the queen began her naming speech.

When the war ended in August 1945, the *Elizabeth* was selected first to be returned to Cunard and restored for luxury commercial service. She would be, in many ways, a symbol of peace and a return to normality. After arriving at Southampton in June 1946, military equipment was removed, and large consignments of furniture and other fittings were unloaded from warehouses throughout Britain. Work went on around the clock. In all, 21,000 separate pieces of furniture were placed aboard, including 4,500 sofas, chairs and tables. There were also 6,000 pairs of curtains and bedspreads, and a further 2,000 carpets. The *Queen Elizabeth* – now over six years old – finally left Southampton, stopped at Cherbourg and then crossed to New York. She is seen here during her post-war maiden arrival in October 1946. She was joined by the *Queen Mary* in the following July, and the two-ship weekly Atlantic express service went into operation. It was immensely successful, hugely profitable and added much to recovering post-war Britain.

This second ship of Cunard's illustrious team, known everywhere simply as the *Queens*, was a more modern ship in several ways than the earlier *Queen Mary*. The *Elizabeth* had two funnels and not three, cleaner upper decks, a raked bow and, within, twelve boilers instead of the twenty-four aboard the *Mary*. Cunard and John Brown had learned much from the French and their innovative, progressive *Normandie*.

Shown here at the Ocean Terminal in Southampton during her peacetime, commercial days, the *Queen Elizabeth* was due to enter service in April 1940, thus creating the world's first two-ship express service. Instead, the war started, and the *Elizabeth* was completed in military gray and went off to America on a secret maiden voyage. She did not receive the initial glamour and high excitement that greeted the *Queen Mary* in May 1936.

The *Queen Elizabeth* has often been referred to as one of the most beautiful-looking liners ever built. After fleeing to the safety of neutral America, to Pier 90 in New York, she was pressed into valiant Allied troop service, carrying up to 15,000 soldier-passengers each voyage. There had been a plan, although a brief one, to rebuild her as the world's largest aircraft carrier – carrying 270 aircraft in her vast innards in one plan or, in another scheme, carrying forty-eight aircraft along with 6,000 troops.

The *Queens* were the most spectacularly profitable pair of liners ever built and headed the great Cunard fleet, which numbered twelve liners by 1957. The Line was said to carry one-third of all Atlantic seagoing passengers during the 1950s. The *Queen Elizabeth* was typically a three-class liner, carrying 2,233 passengers in total – 823 first class, 662 cabin class and 798 tourist class. A suite in first class was priced from $1,200, while dogs traveled in the upper-deck kennels for $25.

Occasionally, even the mighty *Queens* had their troubles. The *Elizabeth* went aground near Southampton in 1949, the *Mary* was tossed about in 1956 in one of the Atlantic's worst storms, and on a foggy summer's day in 1959 the *Elizabeth* collided with a freighter outside New York harbor. There were also dockers' strikes, when passengers had to handle their own luggage, and tug strikes, when the liners had to dock and undock themselves. On winter crossings, there was often fierce weather, as seen in this view from the port side bridge wing. The *Queens* might be delayed and then arrive hours behind schedule.

Right: Seen here arriving at Port Everglades, Florida, in November 1968, the *Queen Elizabeth* was to become the US East Coat version of the *Queen Mary* along the West Coast. The refitted *Elizabeth* was to be a hotel, museum and collection of restaurants and shops, but the entire project was snarled in serious financial problems. Instead, the Cunard liner (the Company held an 85 per cent share in this project) sat idle – rusting, sun-scorched and mostly neglected. She went to auction in September 1970, was sold to Taiwanese-based shipping tycoon C. Y. Tung, and was to be refitted as the floating university cruise ship *Seawise University*. After $6 million of changes done while lying in Hong Kong harbor, the former *Elizabeth* was to depart for dry docking in Japan when, on 9 January 1972, fires broke out aboard. Fireboats and other craft poured far too much water on the burning ship and so, on the following day, she capsized and became a total loss. She was dismantled where she lay, her remains carted off, and today the sight is landfilled and used as a container port.

THE SUPERLINER WAY
TO and FROM
EUROPE
QUEEN MARY   QUEEN ELIZABETH

Opposite: Twilight times! Shown here at New York in a view from 1962, the brand new *France* is on the left and the *Mauretania* in the center. The *Queen Elizabeth* and her running mate began to lose money in the early sixties. The airlines were an unbeatable rival. Both *Queens* were sent on periodic cruises, five days from New York to Nassau and seven nights from Southampton to Las Palmas, as money-making alternatives. In 1965–66, the *Elizabeth* was actually extensively refitted and modernized, being fitted with a lido deck, outdoor pool, complete air-conditioning and with private bathroom facilities in far more cabins. However, she was an aging ship, expensive to operate and sail competitively, and continued to show great losses. While it was planned to keep the refitted *Elizabeth* in service until as late as 1975, the *Mary* was retired in September 1967, and the *Elizabeth* followed in October 1968.

MEDIA (1947)

The 13,500-ton sisters *Media* (seen arriving on her maiden voyage in New York's Upper Bay in August 1947) and *Parthia* were unique to the post-Second World War Cunard fleet. They were the Company's only combination liners, carrying 250 all first-class passengers as well as six holds of freight. They were originally designed as twelve-passenger freighters in 1946 for the Brocklebank Line, a Cunard subsidiary. But soon after construction began, plans were changed and the designs reworked. As combination liners, Cunard managers felt, the pair would be ideal for monthly New York–Liverpool sailings. When the 530-foot-long *Media* first arrived in New York, she was notable – the ship was the first brand-new passenger ship to be ordered following the war. Notably, they were also very poor 'sea boats' and so, in 1952, the *Media* was the first Cunarder to be fitted with fin stabilizers. Quite successful, they were soon also installed aboard the mighty *Queens*.

PARTHIA (1948)

The *Media* and *Parthia* (shown here departing from New York) were club-like (uniquely for the time, every cabin had a private bathroom), comfortable, but largely successful. Because of their passenger and cargo balance, they spent long periods in port turnarounds and were therefore costly. The *Media* was sold off in 1961, becoming the Italian liner *Flavia*; the *Parthia* became the *Remuera* for New Zealand Shipping Co., and later the *Aramac* for the Eastern & Australian Steamship Co.

CARONIA (1948)

Soon after the war ended in 1945, Cunard began planning for another major liner for Atlantic service. Such a new ship would be similar in size to the 1939-built *Mauretania*. Then, in a flash of inspiration, Company directors caught a glimpse of the future and totally redesigned the liner for long, luxurious, revenue-earning cruises. Her keel plates were laid down in 1946 and in the following year, in October, Princess Elizabeth (later HM the Queen) did the naming at the John Brown yard at Clydebank. The 34,100-grt *Caronia* was very significant – she was the biggest British liner to be built since the end of the war, and the government used the ship as a great symbol of national recovery. Seen here on her trials, the *Caronia* also ranked as the largest single-stack liner in the world.

The 715-foot-long *Caronia* – distinctively painted in several shades of green and so given the dubbing of 'Green Goddess' – had a number of design innovations for Cunard. She was the first big Company liner to have private facilities in every cabin, and had a permanent outdoor pool. While she would undertake very occasional crossings between Southampton and New York (carrying first- as well as cabin-class passengers), the 940-passenger *Caronia* was used from the start in cruising, mostly on long, luxurious cruises.

The *Caronia* had a very loyal following – passengers who came voyage after voyage, year after year. One lady is in fact still the all-time champion of cruising – she spent fourteen years aboard the luxurious Cunarder.

The ship, with a reduced cruising capacity of 600 (down from 900) and often only at 300–400 passengers, was like a seagoing club. 'It was all luxury – great food, superb service and deep pampering,' remembered one passenger from the 1950s. The ship had an established pattern: a three-month long cruise, usually around the world, in winter; a six-week spring cruise around the Mediterranean; forty-five nights in summer to Scandinavia and the North Cape; and then six to eight weeks in autumn in the Mediterranean and Black seas.

The *Caronia*'s itinerary for her World Cruise, departing from New York on 27 January 1964, read: Port Everglades, Trinidad, Rio de Janeiro, Cape Town, Durban, Tamatave, Port Louis, Port Victoria, Bombay, Colombo, Singapore, Bangkok, Hong Kong, Kobe, Yokohama, Honolulu, Long Beach, Acapulco, Balboa and Cristobal. It all took ninety-five days and was priced from $2,850.

Seen here at Wellington, New Zealand, in February 1951, the *Caronia* was soon rated as 'the most luxurious liner afloat'. Even to some Cunard loyalists, she was said to be superior to first class aboard the celebrated *Queens*. The *Caronia* had an extraordinary ratio of 640 crew members to her 600 cruise passengers. 'The crew gave her a competitive edge,' reported a former senior officer. 'The crew made her. They were mostly older, highly trained, very loyal staff members. The *Caronia* was an extremely desirable assignment among Cunard crew. During long cruises, as an example, stewards and stewardesses would welcome the returning passengers with stateroom tea for the ladies, cocktails for the gentlemen and then draw their hot baths. It was in ways like coming home to a grand country house.'

Shown arriving at Cape Town, with Table Mountain in the background, the *Caronia*'s sparkle began to dim in the early 1960s. New, smarter luxury ships were entering the long-cruise market – ships such as the *Gripsholm*, *Kungsholm*, *Sagafjord* and *Rotterdam*. Although she was the Company's 'prestige ship', she was becoming far too expensive and so, in the great downsizing of 1967–68, the *Caronia* was withdrawn. Sold to Greek interests and renamed *Caribia* for intended New York–Caribbean operations, her new career was marked by deep financial problems, and instead she loitered around New York harbor in idleness. Clouded in debt, she was finally auctioned off to Taiwanese scrappers and left New York under tow, in April 1974, for demolition. However, while seeking refuge at Guam from an August tropical storm, the tug lost control, the towlines snapped and the ex-*Caronia* was thrown against a rocky breakwater and broke in three pieces. Local authorities rushed in and had the remains dismantled on the spot.

SAXONIA/CARMANIA (1954)

Based somewhat on the previous design of the *Caronia*, Cunard turned to an old friend, John Brown & Company Limited at Clydebank, for the construction of a pair, and then changed to a quartet of liners for the UK–Canada service. In fact, they would be the biggest liners for Cunard's alternate Canadian service – but also the Company's very last full-time Atlantic liners. These 22,000-ton ships had balanced passenger and cargo capacities, single-domed funnels, accommodations for about 900 passengers in two classes and seven hatches for freight. They were named *Saxonia* (1954), *Ivernia* (1955), *Carinthia* (1956) and *Sylvania* (1957). The only negative was in fact rather serious in the face of future demands – these ships were not designed to cruise as an alternate to sluggish winters on the Atlantic and the onslaught of competitive jet aircraft in the sixties.

The first of the series, the 608-foot-long *Saxonia* was launched by Lady Churchill on 17 February 1954. The ship entered service the following September.

The *Saxonia*, together with the *Ivernia* – with accommodations divided between 125 in first class and 800 in tourist – sailed between Southampton, Le Havre, Quebec City and Montreal. In deep winter, when the St Lawrence was ice-choked, these ships added London to their itineraries and sailed to Halifax, then onward to New York. Cunard offered the two-night passages between Halifax and New York for $25 in tourist-class quarters.

Because of their large cargo capacities, the *Saxonia* and her three sisters had long turnarounds in port. At New York during their wintertime calls, these ships would often arrive on Saturdays and then depart six days later on Fridays. This made them, of course, expensive ships to maintain. In this view, the *Saxonia* is docked as the *Sylvania* departs.

THE NEW CUNARD LINER "SAXONIA" 22,000 TONS

Cunard selected the *Saxonia* and *Ivernia* for complete refits in 1962–63. They went back to their builders on the Clyde, and were refitted for cruising. They were repainted in white, given private bathrooms in all cabins and had their aft cargo hatches replaced by an outdoor pool and lido deck. The ships were even given new identities: the *Saxonia* became the *Carmania* (seen here at Madeira) while the *Ivernia* changed to *Franconia*.

IVERNIA/FRANCONIA (1955)

The *Ivernia* and her three sisters were scheduled as a team, making weekly departures, with a round trip for each ship per month. They were intended to be much alike, but had some modifications while under construction. One officer later remembered, 'The *Saxonia* and *Ivernia* were intended to be "new" Cunarders and were actually more modern, even quite flashy in decor and lacked what many passengers felt was a Cunard standard of decoration.'

Among the cargos carried westbound aboard Cunarders such as the *Ivernia* were British-manufactured goods, woolens and whiskies. Occasionally there were special items such as race cars and Rolls-Royces.

CARINTHIA (1956)

The second identical pair of this foursome were the *Carinthia* (seen arriving on her maiden arrival to Montreal in June 1956) and *Sylvania* (added in June 1957), which sailed on an alternate service – between Liverpool, Greenock, Quebec City and Montreal (skipping Greenock, but traveling via Cobh to Halifax and New York in winter).

Accommodations aboard the *Carinthia* (shown here at Pier 92, New York) and *Sylvania* were slightly different than the earlier pier, carrying 154 in first class and approximately 725 in tourist class.

SYLVANIA (1957)

'The decor aboard the *Carinthia* and *Sylvania* was revised from the earlier pair and was superior in taste and styling,' according to one Cunard officer. 'They more like traditional Cunard – warm, inviting, altogether with lots more brown-colored woods. In fact, there were even some historic touches – the chairs in the first class restaurant aboard the Carinthia were actually brought from storage after having been on the *Aquitania* of 1914.'

By the mid-1960s, the transatlantic liner trade was in deep decline. Cunard was faced with changing times, much decreased passenger loads and significant losses. The Company was also faced with a far different future – one that included far more cruising. In 1965, ships such as the 875-passenger *Sylvania* – seen here in the Mersey – sometimes crossed with as few as 200–300 passengers aboard.

Ships such as the *Sylvania* were sent on more and more cruises – from Southampton or Liverpool, for example, to the Mediterranean, Spain and Portugal, West Africa and the Atlantic Isles. Cruises in 1966 included twelve nights from Liverpool to Madeira, Las Palmas, Tenerife and Lisbon from £89 and far longer twenty-eight days to the Mediterranean from Southampton from £210.

Changing names! Later painted in 'cruising white', the *Sylvania* and *Carinthia* were finally sold off in 1968. They had long and diverse successive careers. The *Sylvania* went on to become *Fairwind*, *Sitmar Fairwind*, *Dawn Princess*, *Albatros* and finally, for her trip to the breakers in 2003, the *Genoa*; the *Carinthia* later sailed as the *Fairsea*, *Fair Princess*, *China Sea Discovery* and, for a last voyage to the scrappers in 2005–06, the *Discovery*. As for the *Saxonia/Carmania* and *Ivernia/Franconia*, these ships were sold off in 1973, becoming the Soviet *Leonid Sobinov* and *Feodor Shalyapin* respectively. The ex-*Saxonia/Carmania* was scrapped in 1999, the former *Ivernia/Franconia* in 2004.

In the great changes and vast rethinking of the 1960s, Cunard thought of a more traditional three-class superliner, dubbed the *Q3*, as a replacement for the aging *Queen Mary*. This was rethought, however, and changed to a two-class, 65,000-ton liner that would be launched on 20 September 1967 at Clydebank as the *Queen Elizabeth 2*. After some teething problems, which caused several delays, the 963-foot-long *QE2* finally entered service in May 1969. Dubbed by one member of the press as 'Britain's biggest white elephant', the ship was criticized at first as misplaced, a money-loser, and anachronistic. Seen here at New York Piers 84 and 86 with the *France* and *Michelangelo* in a view from February 1973, the *QE2* settled down to a happy, quite successful and even profitable life. Cunard sensibly made friends with the airlines and offered thoughtful travel arrangements on the North Atlantic – one way by sea, the other way by air.

Converted to diesel drive in a massive refit in 1986–87, the *QE2* now had an added distinction: the last steamship on the Atlantic. By the time she was retired from Cunard service (in November 2008), she was not just seen as successful, but very successful – she had, in her thirty-nine years, carried more passengers, steamed more miles, visited more ports and most likely made more money than any big liner in history. Even in being sold to buyers in Dubai for $100 million, she changed hands for a record price. She was hardly the end of Cunard, which was bought by Miami-headquartered Carnival Corporation in 1998, and led to the 151,000-ton *Queen Mary 2* in 2003, the 90,000-ton *Queen Victoria* in 2007 and then the 92,000-ton *Queen Elizabeth* in 2010.

The Cunard house flag continues to wave – and wave proudly!

BIBLIOGRAPHY

Braynard, Frank O. and William H. Miller, *Fifty Famous Liners* Vols 1–3 (Cambridge, England: Patrick Stephens Ltd, 1982–86).

Crowdy, Michael and Kevin O'Donoghue (eds), *Marine News* (Kendal, Cumbria: World Ship Society, 1963–2014).

Devol, George and Thomas Cassidy (eds), *Ocean & Cruise News* (Stamford, Connecticut: World Ocean & Cruise Liner Society, 1980–2014).

Fielding, Temple, *Fielding's Travel Guide to Europe* (New York: William Sloane Associates, 1964).

Haws, Duncan, *Merchant Fleets: Cunard Line* (Hereford: TCL Publications, 1987).

Mayes, William, *Cruise Ships* (revised edition) (Windsor: Overview Press Ltd, 2009).

Miller, William H., *British Ocean Liners: A Twilight Era 1960–85* (New York: W. W. Norton & Co., 1986).

Miller, William H., *Floating Palaces: The Great Atlantic Liners* (Stroud, Gloucestershire: Amberley Publishing, 2011).

Miller, William H., *Great British Passenger Ships* (Stroud, Gloucestershire: The History Press, 2010).

Miller, William H., *Pictorial Encyclopedia of Ocean Liners 1864–1994* (Mineola, New York: Dover Publications Inc., 1995).

Miller, William H., *Picture History of British Ocean Liners* (Mineola, New York: Dover Publications Inc., 2001).

Miller, William H., *Picture History of the Cunard Line 1840–1990* (Mineola, New York: Dover Publications Inc., 1991).

Miller, William H., *Under the Red Ensign: British Passenger Liners of the 1950s & '60s* (Stroud, Gloucestershire: The History Press, 2009).

Newall, Peter, *Cunard Line: A Fleet History* (Longton, Preston, England: Ships in Focus Publications, 2012).

Official Steamship Guide (New York: Transportation Guides Inc., 1937–63.)

ACKNOWLEDGMENTS

The authors wish to thank Amberley Publishing, and specifically Campbell McCutcheon, Louis Archard and Chris Skal, for creating this book. Further appreciation to Richard Faber, Michael Hadgis and Anthony La Forgia. Thank you, too, to Vitaly Logvinenko, for his wise advice about colorizing the photographs for this book. Thank you to Janette McCutcheon for access to her super collection of images. And, of course, thanks to the Cunard Line itself.